P9-CCP-335

Lives and Times

Clarence Birdseye

Tiffany Peterson

Heinemann Library
Chicago, Illinois

© 2003 Heinemann Library
a division of Reed Elsevier Inc.
Chicago, Illinois

Customer Service 888-454-2279

Visit our website at www.heinemannlibrary.com

All rights reserved. No part of this publication may be reproduced or transmitted in any form or by any means, electronic or mechanical, including photocopying, recording, taping, or any information storage and retrieval system, without permission in writing from the publisher.

Designed by Herman Adler Design
Illustrations by Yoshi Miyake, Map by Mapping Specialists
Printed and bound by Lake Book Manufacturing, Inc.

07 06 05 04 03
10 9 8 7 6 5 4 3 2 1

Library of Congress Cataloging-in-Publication Data
Peterson, Tiffany.
  Clarence Birdseye / Tiffany Peterson.
      p. cm. -- (Lives and times)
Summary: Introduces the life of Clarence Birdseye, who invented a quick-freeze method to preserve the fresh flavor of food and founded the Birds Eye Frosted Foods company in 1929.
Includes bibliographical references and index.
  ISBN 1-4034-3247-3 (hardcover, library binding) -- ISBN 1-4034-4255-X (pbk.)
  1. Birdseye, Clarence, 1886-1956--Juvenile literature. 2. Frozen foods industry--United States--History--Juvenile literature. 3. Inventors--United States--Biography--Juvenile literature. 4. Industrialists--United States--Biography--Juvenile literature. [1. Birdseye, Clarence, 1886-1956. 2. Food industry and trade. 3. Inventors. 4. Industrialists.] I. Title. II. Lives and times (Des Plaines, Ill.)
  HD9217.U52B577 2003
  338.7'66402853'092--dc21

2003001522

Acknowledgments
The author and publishers are grateful to the following for permission to reproduce copyright material: pp. 1, 5, 28 Brian Warling/Heinemann Library; p. 4 Japack Company/Corbis; pp. 6, 9, 20, 22, 24 Brown Brothers; p. 7 Photodisc, Inc.; p. 8 Amherst College; pp. 11, 14, 15 The Peary-MacMillan Arctic Museum/Bowdoin College; pp. 12, 13 North Wind Picture Archives; p. 16 Galen Rowell/Corbis; pp.18, 25 Bettmann/Corbis; p. 21 Teich Company Collection/Lake County Discovery Museum; pp. 23, 29 Agrilink Foods; p. 26 Pablo Corral/Corbis; p. 27 Everett Collection

Cover photographs by Brian Warling/Heinemann Library and Agrilink Foods

Photo research by Carol Parden.

Special thanks to Michelle Rimsa for her comments in the preparation of this book.

Every effort has been made to contact copyright holders of any material reproduced in this book. Any omissions will be rectified in subsequent printings if notice is given to the publisher.

Some words are shown in bold, **like this.** You can find out what they mean by looking in the glossary.

Contents

BIRDS EYE.

Frozen Fresh Foods

People need and want to eat vegetables all year.

Eating vegetables helps people stay healthy. Many vegetables are grown in the United States, such as green beans and corn. Most of them are ripe in summer and fall.

Clarence Birdseye found a way to freeze foods so they still taste fresh. With frozen foods, people can have vegetables, fruits, and other foods any time of year.

These frozen foods can be stored in the freezer for months.

Early Years

Clarence Birdseye was born in 1886 in Brooklyn, New York. When he was a teenager, his family moved to Montclair, New Jersey.

This is how Brooklyn looked when Clarence lived there.

In Montclair, Clarence tried many new things. One thing he learned was the skill of **taxidermy.** In high school, he took a cooking class to learn other skills.

Clarence learned how to stuff animals. He could make them look almost like they did when they were alive.

College and Work

In 1908, Clarence went to Amherst College in Massachusetts. He learned more about animals in his **biology** classes. College cost a lot of money, though. Clarence needed money to pay for school.

One way young Clarence made money was by catching frogs. He sold them to the Bronx Zoo in New York. They were fed to snakes.

In 1910, Clarence ran out of money for school. He left college. For a short time, he worked in an office in New York City. He also worked as a **field naturalist.**

Clarence did many small jobs for people while he lived in New York. This is how the city looked at that time.

Fur Trading

Clarence wanted to use what he had learned about animals in his jobs. So, he decided to become a **fur trader.** In 1912, he went to Labrador, in Canada.

Clarence spent four years traveling around northern Canada selling furs.

During the short, hot summers, Clarence traveled by boat to trade furs. In the long, cold winters, he traveled on a dogsled.

The easiest way for people to travel over the snow in Labrador was by dogsled.

BIRDS EYE®

A Family of His Own

In 1915, Clarence went home for a visit. While there, he married Eleanor Gannett. When he returned to Labrador to work, Eleanor stayed behind. She was going to have their first of four children.

In 1916, Clarence's wife and their new baby son joined Clarence in snowy Labrador.

Clarence worried about his family during Labrador's cold winter.

Clarence wanted to be sure that his new family always had enough to eat. He needed to find a way to store food so it would not rot.

BIRDS EYE.

Frozen Fish

One day, Clarence watched the local **Inuit** ice fishing. They pulled fish through a hole in the ice. As the fish came out of the cold, salty water, they quickly froze.

The fish that the Inuit caught and froze could be stored for months.

Clarence noticed something else. Once cooked, the frozen fish tasted nearly as good as fresh fish.

Clarence learned from the Inuit how best to freeze different foods.

BIRDS EYE

Testing It Out

Clarence thought he could freeze other foods the same way the **Inuit** had frozen fish. He **experimented** with different foods. He froze cabbage and rabbit, duck, and **caribou** meat.

Caribou are large deer that are found in Canada.

With frozen food, Clarence's wife and son had plenty to eat.

Clarence followed the Inuit's example. First, he placed the food in cold salt water. Then, he put it out in the wind. The food froze. And, it tasted fresh when cooked.

BIRDS EYE.

A New Business

In 1917, the United States began fighting in World War I. Clarence decided he should move his family back to the United States.

When the United States went to war, Clarence's ideas about freezing food were put on hold.

Clarence worked for three different U.S. companies during the war. After the war, he went back to **experimenting** with food. He wanted to find new ways to freeze it.

With only seven dollars, Clarence bought salt, ice, and an electric fan.

BIRDS EYE®

Quick-Freezing

Clarence discovered a very good way to freeze food. He called it quick-freezing. Cold metal plates helped to freeze the food. They also pressed the food into small cardboard boxes.

Clarence created this machine to freeze and package foods.

People were used to eating fish fresh from the docks. Clarence knew frozen fish would have to taste just as fresh.

In 1924, Clarence found three people who were interested in his work with quick-freezing. Together, they started General Seafoods Company.

Success!

Clarence understood that people needed food packages that were easy to store in the freezer.

Clarence began selling his frozen foods in small cardboard packages. He sold frozen fish, meat, fruits, and vegetables.

In 1929, General Foods bought Clarence's company. They renamed it "Birds Eye Frosted Foods." Clarence worked for the company. He kept **experimenting** and improving his process.

Birds Eye Frosted Foods were sold throughout the United States.

From Freezing to Drying

Clarence **experimented** with foods such as carrots to improve his dehydration process.

Clarence wanted to find other ways to store foods. He turned to **dehydration.** Like frozen foods, dried foods can be stored for months.

Clarence knew that freezing foods quickly **preserved** their fresh taste. He thought dehydrating quickly would have the same result. After six years of experimenting, Clarence perfected his dehydration process.

Like his frozen foods, Clarence's dehydrated foods were packaged in small boxes.

Lifelong Inventor

Clarence was a millionaire. He did not need to work anymore. He enjoyed **experimenting,** though. So, he kept working on new inventions.

Clarence invented many things, such as a **heat lamp** for keeping food warm.

Only Clarence or someone with his permission could make or sell his patented inventions.

On October 7, 1956, Clarence Birdseye died from heart trouble. By then, he had around 300 **patents.**

BIRDS EYE.

Learning More About Birdseye

Birds Eye still packages frozen foods in small, easy-to-store cardboard boxes or plastic bags.

Clarence Birdseye was not the first person to freeze foods. But his quick-freezing method continues to be the best way to **preserve** fresh flavor.

Today, the company Clarence started is called Birds Eye Foods. The company still works hard to give people fresh tasting frozen foods.

Today, Clarence's name is known around the world.

Fact File

- Clarence Birdseye is known as the "Father of Quick Freezing."

- He liked to play Chinese checkers and to give large dinner parties.

- Clarence always liked experimenting with plants. In Peru, he found a way to make paper out of **sugarcane** stalks.

- Clarence and his wife, Eleanor, worked together to write a book called *Growing Woodland Plants.*

- The Birdseyes had four children—two boys and two girls.

Timeline

December 9, 1886 Clarence Birdseye is born

1912 Clarence becomes a **fur trader** in Labrador, Canada

1915 Clarence marries Eleanor Gannett, after writing letters to her for years

1924 Clarence forms General Seafoods Corporation

1925 Starts selling quick-frozen meat

1929 Birds Eye Frosted Foods company is formed

1932 First Birds Eye vegetables sold in stores

October 7, 1956 Clarence dies from heart trouble

Glossary

biology study of living things, such as plants and animals

caribou large deer that lives in Canada

dehydration drying out food so it can be stored longer

experiment test that is done to discover or prove something

field naturalist one who studies wildlife and the environment

fur trader person who buys and sells animal furs

heat lamp lamp that gets very hot, often used to keep foods warm

Inuit native person of Canada, Alaska, or Greenland; also known as Eskimo

patent legal paper given to a person that says he or she is the only person allowed to make a certain invention unless special permission is given

preserve keep the same

sugarcane tall plant that is used to make sugar

taxidermy process of preparing, stuffing, and mounting dead animals to make them look like they did when they were alive

More Books to Read

Robinson, Fay and Allan Fowler. *Vegetables, Vegetables, Vegetables!* Danbury, Conn.: Children's Press, 2000.

Frost, Helen. *The Vegetable Group.* Mankato, Minn.: Capstone, 2000.

Harper, Charise Mericle. *Imaginative Inventions.* Boston: Little Brown, 2001.

Rondeau, Amanda. *Vegetables Are Vital.* Edina, Minn.: ABDO, 2002.

Index